A Day With

A Day With INSPIRING LEADERS

MOONSTONE

Published in Moonstone
by Rupa Publications India Pvt. Ltd 2023
7/16, Ansari Road, Daryaganj
New Delhi 110002

Sales centres:
Prayagraj Bengaluru Chennai
Hyderabad Jaipur Kathmandu
Kolkata Mumbai

Copyright © Rupa Publications India Pvt. Ltd 2023

All rights reserved.
No part of this publication may be reproduced, transmitted,
or stored in a retrieval system, in any form or by any means,
electronic, mechanical, photocopying, recording or otherwise,
without the prior permission of the publisher.

P-ISBN: 978-93-5520-944-3
E-ISBN: 978-93-5520-919-1

First impression 2023

10 9 8 7 6 5 4 3 2 1

Printed in India
This book is sold subject to the condition that it shall not,
by way of trade or otherwise, be lent, resold, hired out, or otherwise
circulated, without the publisher's prior consent, in any form of binding
or cover other than that in which it is published.

Contents

Nelson Mandela

Meet Frank and Fiona..9

Chapter 1: In Nelson Mandela's House 10

Chapter 2: Apartheid 12

Chapter 3: African National Congress 14

Chapter 4: A Revolutionary 16

Chapter 5: Imprisonment 18

Chapter 6: Freedom 20

Chapter 7: Nobel Prize 22

Chapter 8: President Mandela 24

Chapter 9: Conclusion 26

Timeline 28

Word Meanings 30

Think, Talk and Write 31

What did you learn from Nelson Mandela? 32

What are the five things that you will hange after reading Nelson Mandela's story?...........33

Mahatma Gandhi

Meet Frank and Fiona..35

Chapter 1: In Mahatma Gandhi's Ashram..36

Chapter 2: Early Years..38

Chapter 3: The Barrister..40

Chapter 4: In South Africa 42

Chapter 5: Return to India 44

Chapter 6: Indian National Congress 46

Chapter 7: Non-Violent Revolution 48

Chapter 8: Quit India 50

Chapter 9: Conclusion 52

Timeline 54

Word Meanings 56

Think, Talk and Write 57

What did you learn from Mahatma Gandhi? 58

What are the five things that you will hange after reading Mahatma Gandhi's story? 59

Martin Luther King, Jr.

Meet Frank and Fiona 61

Chapter 1: In Martin Luther King, Jr.'s House 62

Chapter 2: Early Years 64

Chapter 3: Education 66

Chapter 4: The Bus Boycott 68

Chapter 5: Imprisonment 70

Chapter 6: A Famous Speech 72

Chapter 7: A Big Prize 74

Chapter 8: The Author 76

Chapter 9: Conclusion 78

Timeline 80
Word Meanings 82
Think, Talk and Write 83
What did you learn from Martin Luther King, Jr.? 84
What are the five things that you will hange after reading Martin Luther King, Jr.'s story? 85

Mother Teresa

Meet Frank and Fiona..87
Chapter 1: In Mother Teresa's House 88
Chapter 2: A Young Nun 90
Chapter 3: A Teacher 92
Chapter 4: The Divine Call 94
Chapter 5: Missionaries of Charity 96
Chapter 6: Home for the Dying 98
Chapter 7: Around the World 100
Chapter 8: Nobel Prize 102
Chapter 9: Conclusion 104
Timeline 106
Word Meanings 108
Think, Talk and Write 109
What did you learn from Mother Teresa? 110
What are the five things that you will hange after reading Mother Teresa's story? 111
Work Space 112

A Day With
Nelson Mandela

Nelson Mandela was a great leader.
He made South Africa a democracy.
Read on to learn about his life and work.

Meet Frank and Fiona

Chapter 1: In Nelson Mandela's House

Nelson Mandela was born in **Mvezo, South Africa** on 18 July, 1918. He was a great **leader** and **activist**. He became the first Black President of South Africa.

Chapter 2: Apartheid

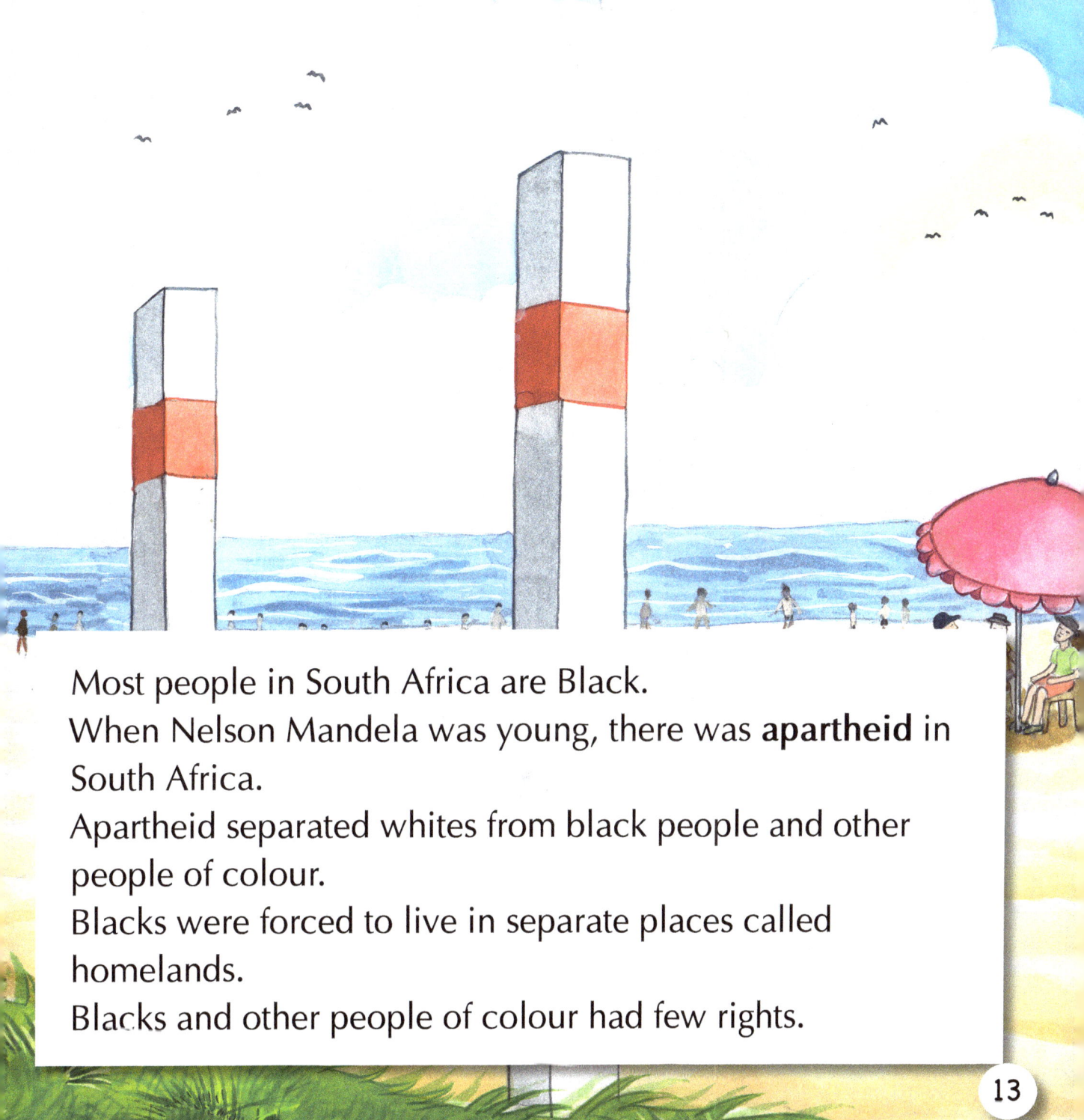

Most people in South Africa are Black.
When Nelson Mandela was young, there was **apartheid** in South Africa.
Apartheid separated whites from black people and other people of colour.
Blacks were forced to live in separate places called homelands.
Blacks and other people of colour had few rights.

Chapter 3: African National Congress

At that time, the African National Congress was fighting for the rights of Black people.
Nelson Mandela wanted rights and freedom for his people.
So, he joined the African National Congress.

Mandela was also a lawyer.
He wanted to help Black people.
So, he gave free or low-cost legal advice to many blacks.

Chapter 4: A Revolutionary

Nelson Mandela led many protests against the government.
In the beginning, he did not believe in violence.
Later, he realized that peaceful struggle could not succeed.
So, he found an armed wing of the African National Congress.
It was known as *uMkhonto we Sizwe* or "Spear of the Nation".
This made him unpopular with the government.
The *uMkhonto we Sizwe* was **banned**.
Mandela had to go into hiding.

Nelson Mandela was arrested after hiding for 17 months. In 1964, he was sentenced to life imprisonment. He was sent to a jail on **Robben Island**. He remained there for the next 18 years.
In 1982, he was sent to the **Pollsmoor Prison**.
Mandela spent 27 years in jail.

Chapter 6: Freedom

Many people all over the world wanted Nelson Mandela to be freed.
They even had a slogan, which was "Free Nelson Mandela!"
On 11 February, 1990, he was released from prison.
The event was broadcast live all over the world.

Nelson Mandela won a big prize in 1993.
It was the Nobel Peace Prize.
He won it for peacefully ending apartheid in South Africa.

Chapter 8: President Mandela

Nelson Mandela wanted South Africa to be a **democracy**.
He wanted all the people to have equal rights.
This made him popular even among the whites.
The people of South Africa made him their president.

Nelson Mandela is an **ambassador** of peace.
He is an **icon** of freedom and equality all over the world.

Mandela died in Johannesburg, South Africa on 5 December, 2013.

Timeline

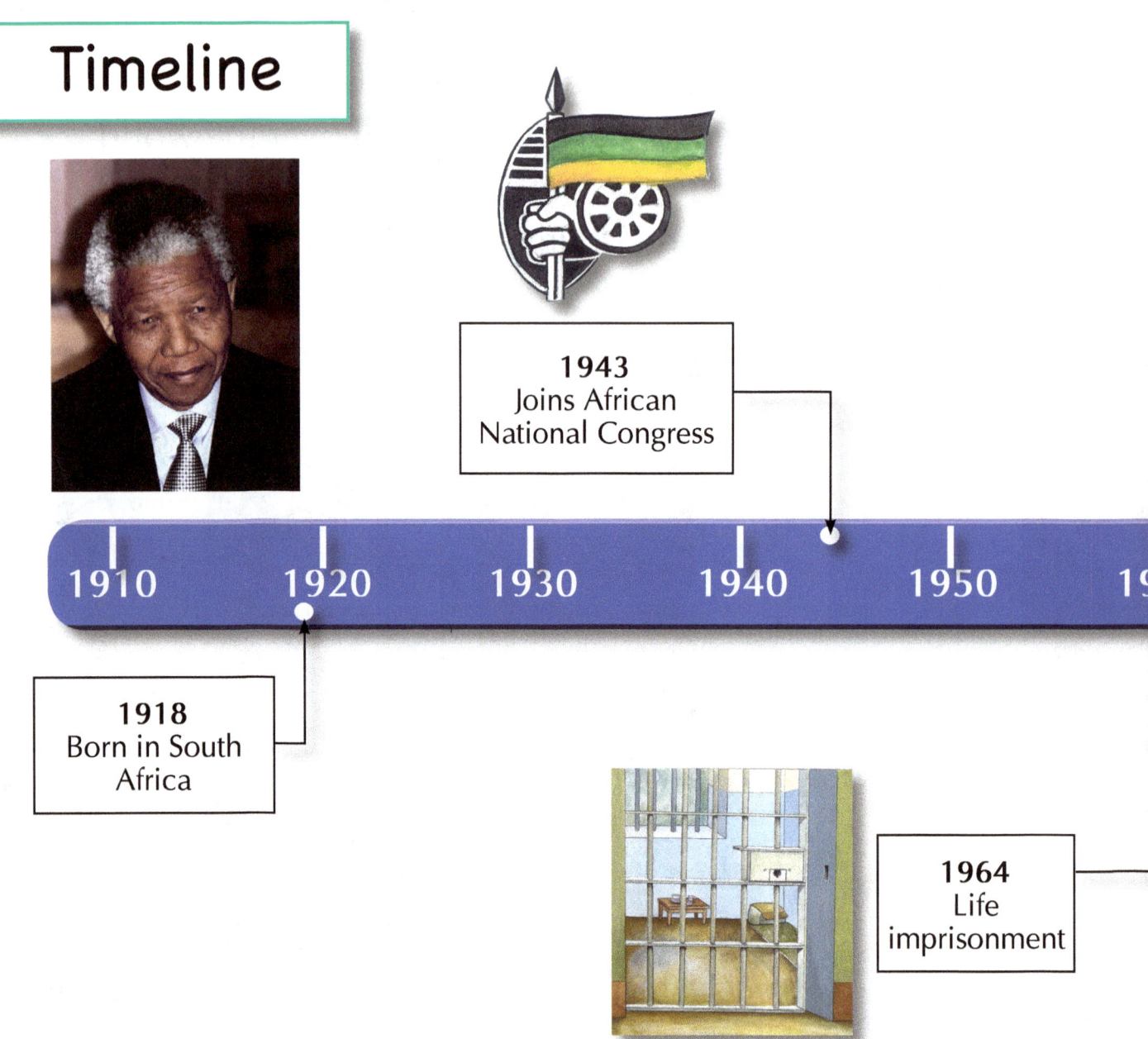

Nelson Mandela's Life and Work

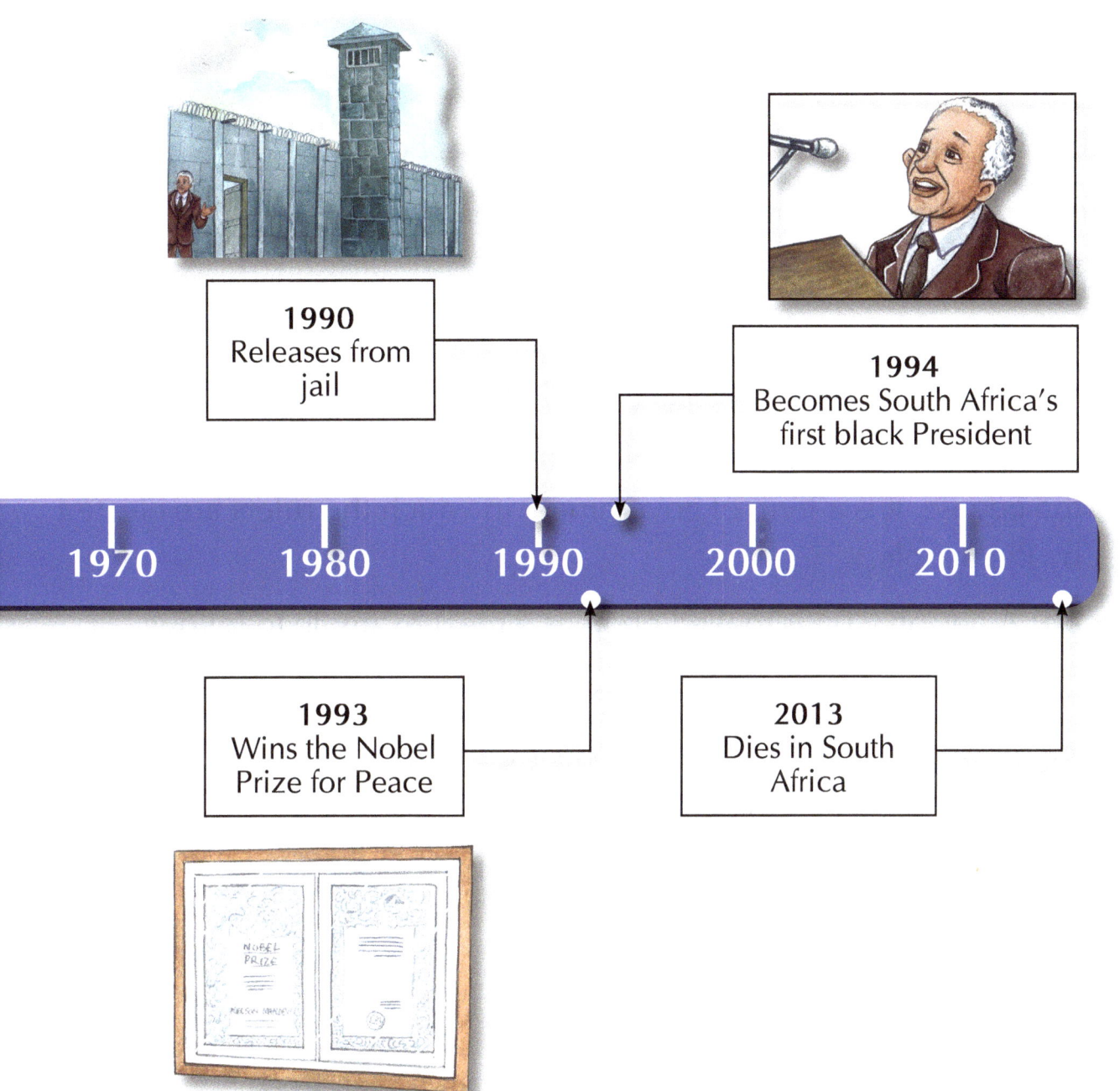

Word Meanings

Activist: A person who works to make things better

Ambassador: A person who is a messenger

Apartheid: An official policy that separates Black people from White people

Ban: An official order making something illegal

Democracy: Democracy is a rule of the people, for the people and by the people. It is a form of government in which the rulers are elected by the people.

Icon: A person who is looked upon as a great example to follow

Leader: A person who leads others

Pollsmoor Prison: A harsh prison near Cape Town, a city in south-western South Africa

Robben Island: An island near Cape Town

South Africa: A country in Africa

Think, Talk and Write

Think About It

Nelson Mandela believed in a dream. He wanted to make South Africa a democracy. What dream do you have for your country? Why? Think about it and try to to explain your dream.

Talk About It

How would you describe Mandela? Tell a partner about him, what he did and how he helped other Black people.

Write About It

Mandela believed that all humans are equal. Write about other people who thought like him.

What did you learn from Nelson Mandela?

What are the five things that you will change after reading Nelson Mandela's story?

A Day With
Mahatma Gandhi

Mahatma Gandhi was a great leader.
He led a non-violent revolution to free India from Great Britain.
Read on to learn about his life and work.

Mahatma Gandhi was born in Porbandar, **India** on 2 October, 1869.
His name, when he was born, was Mohandas Karamchand Gandhi.
He was a great leader and thinker.

At school, Gandhi was very shy.
He was an average student.
But he was very honest and truthful.

At home, Gandhi was an obedient boy.
He loved to serve his parents.

When Gandhi was 18, he went to **England**.
He lived in **London** for the next three years.
He studied law at the **Inner Temple**.
He became a **barrister**.

Chapter 4: In South Africa

In 1893, Gandhi went to South Africa.
There were many Indians in South Africa.
But Indians and other people of colour had few rights compared to Europeans.

This was because there was **racism** in South Africa.

Gandhi decided to fight for the rights of Indians living in South Africa.
He founded the **Natal Indian Congress** in 1894.
He led many protests against the government.
He was beaten and sent to prison, but finally, the government agreed to Gandhi's demands.

People in India heard about Gandhi's struggle in South Africa.
They were inspired by his sacrifice.
In 1915, Gandhi returned to India.
He found himself very popular.
People celebrated his arrival.
They saw him as their new leader.

Chapter 6: Indian National Congress

The **Indian National Congress** was fighting to free India from the British Government.
Gandhi joined the Congress.
He refused to obey the British government.
He led many non-violent protests.
Soon, he became a big leader.

Gandhi did not believe in violence.
He was against any form of cruelty.
Gandhi loved his country.
He wanted to free India from British rule.
But he wanted to lead a non-violent revolution.
He wanted to use **non-violence** as a weapon against the British.

Gandhi started many mass protests against the British. One of his famous protests was called the Quit India Movement. He wanted the British to leave India immediately.

Gandhi was arrested and sent to prison many times. Finally, the protests were successful, and the British were forced to leave India.
In 1947, India became a free country.

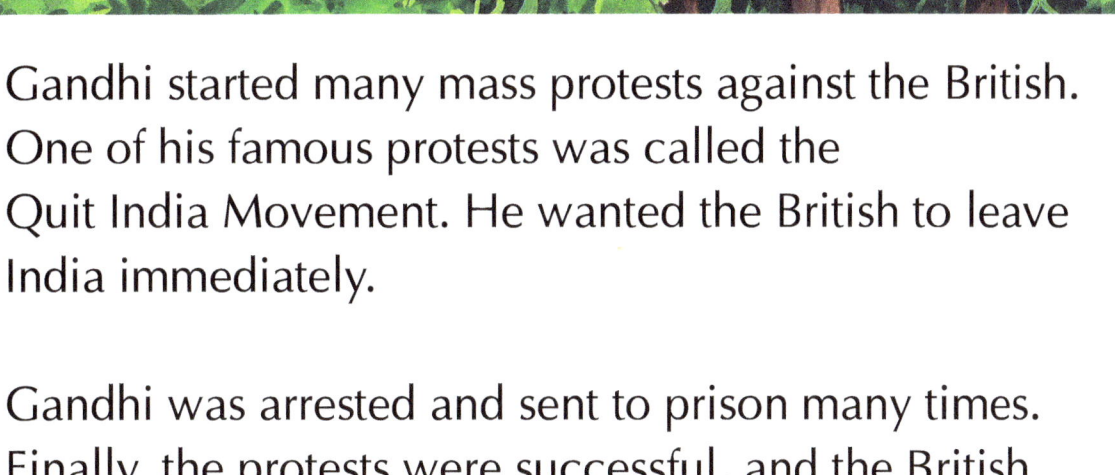

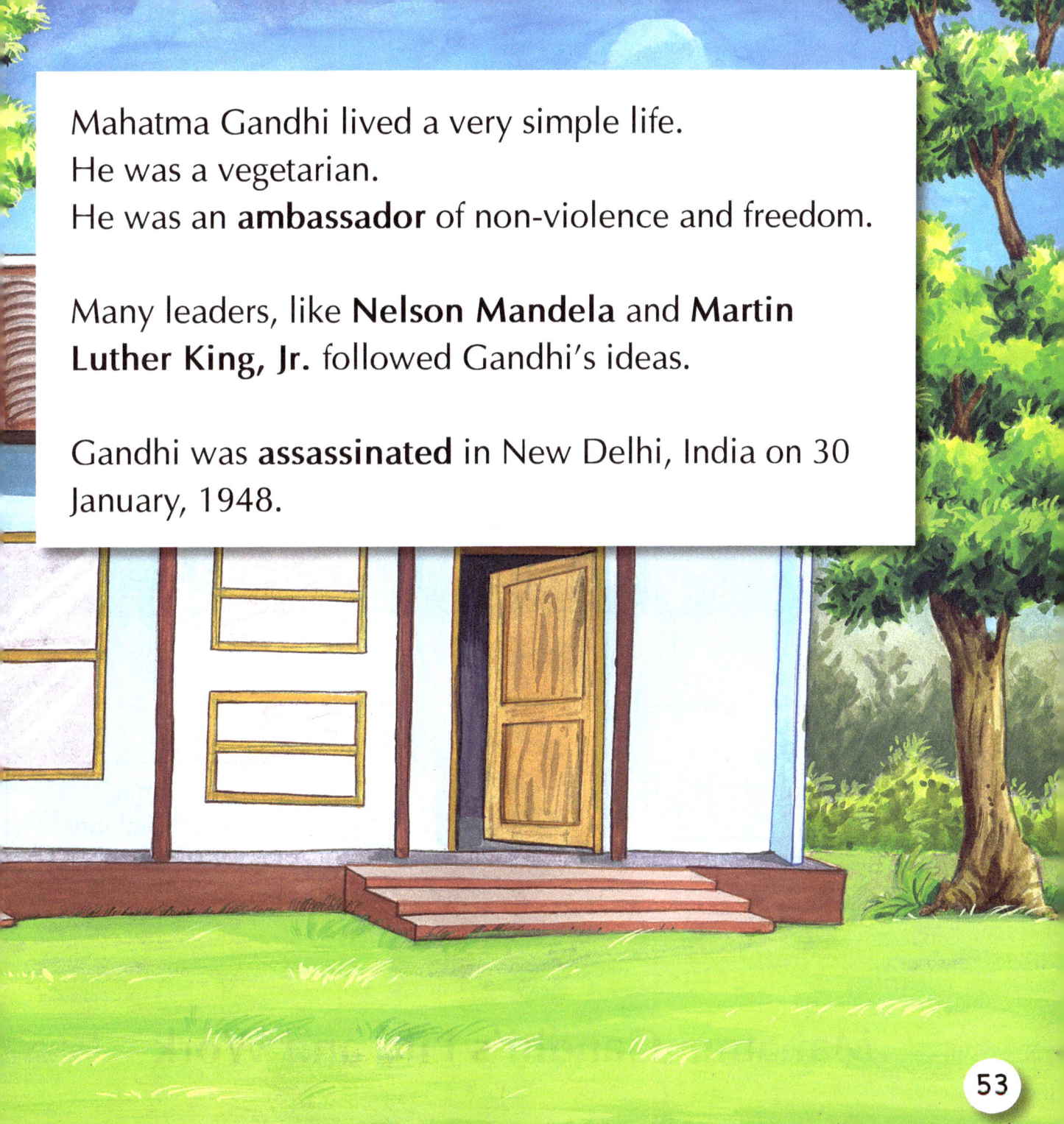

Mahatma Gandhi lived a very simple life.
He was a vegetarian.
He was an **ambassador** of non-violence and freedom.

Many leaders, like **Nelson Mandela** and **Martin Luther King, Jr.** followed Gandhi's ideas.

Gandhi was **assassinated** in New Delhi, India on 30 January, 1948.

Timeline

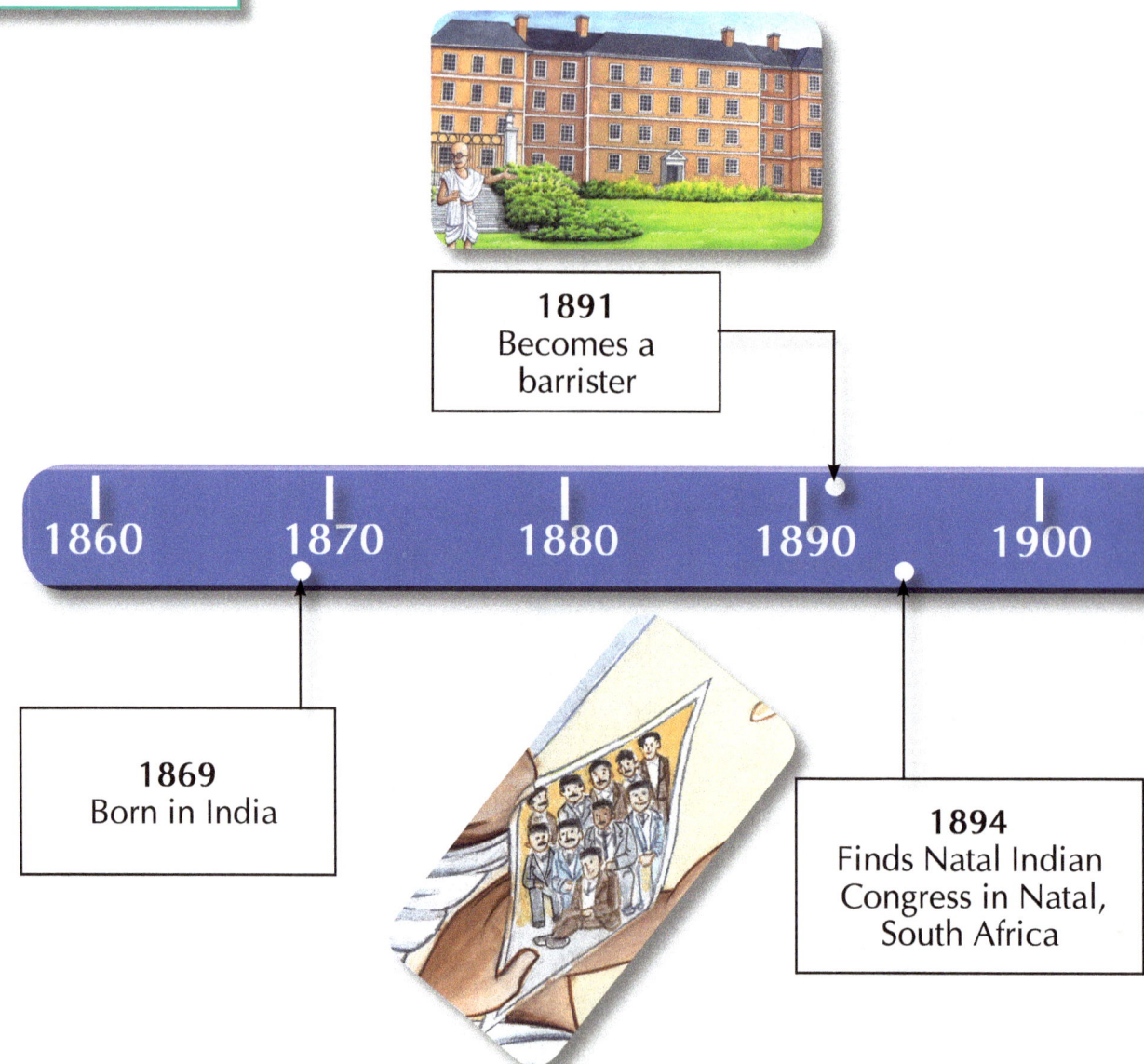

1891
Becomes a barrister

| 1860 | 1870 | 1880 | 1890 | 1900 |

1869
Born in India

1894
Finds Natal Indian Congress in Natal, South Africa

Mahatma Gandhi's Life and Work

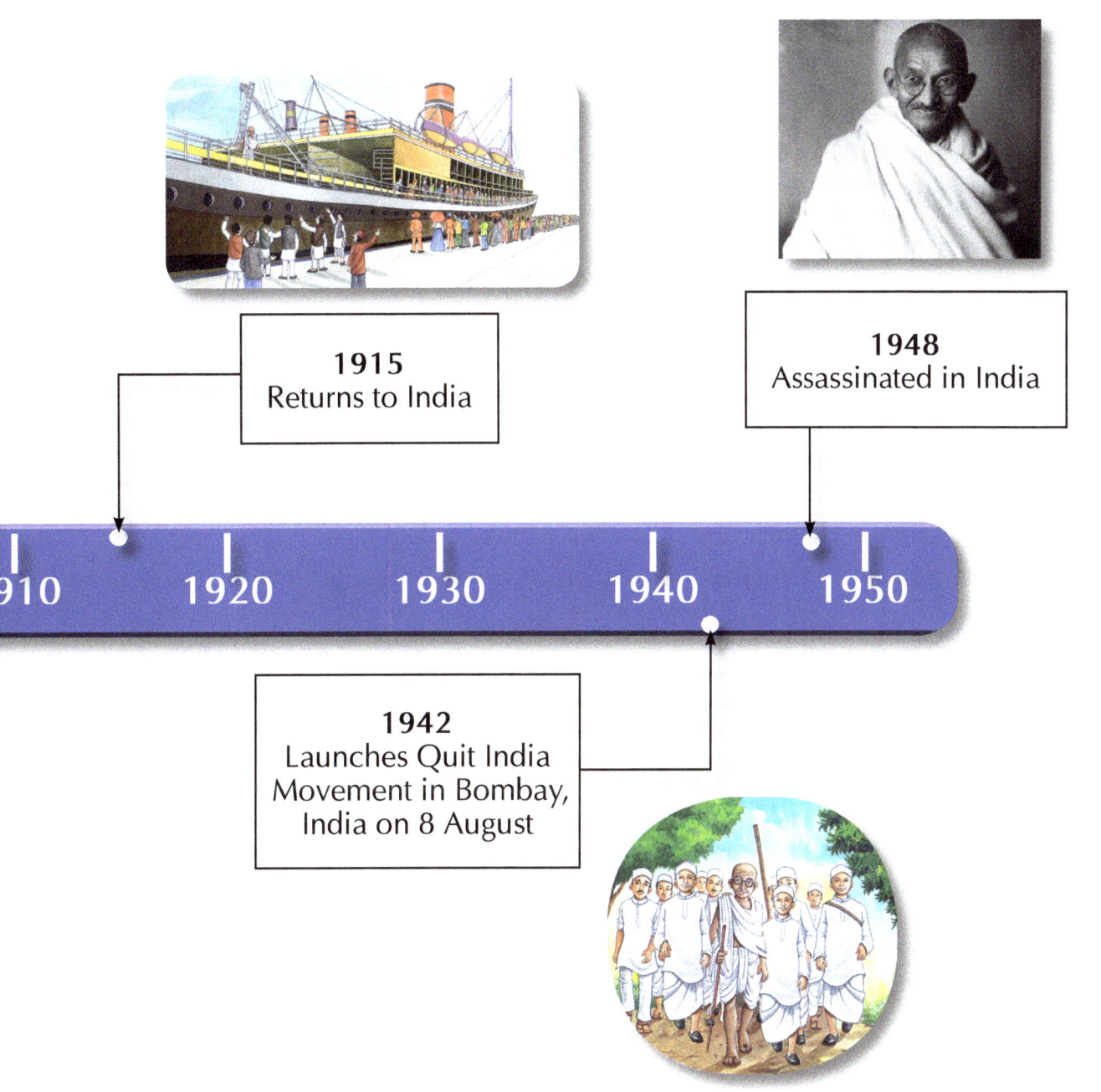

1915
Returns to India

1948
Assassinated in India

1910　1920　1930　1940　1950

1942
Launches Quit India Movement in Bombay, India on 8 August

Word Meanings

Ashram: A place in isolation where a community of people lead a simple life and meditate

Assassinated: To murder a famous or important person, especially for political reasons

Barrister: A lawyer qualified to work in the English Court

England: Part of the United Kingdom, a country in Europe

India: A country in South Asia

Indian National Congress: A political party in India, founded in 1885

Inner Temple: A famous law society in London to study and practice law

London: A city in England. London is the capital of the United Kingdom

Martin Luther King, Jr.: An African-American leader and activist in the United States of America

Natal Indian Congress: An association founded by Gandhi in South Africa

Non-Violence: A method to bring about social change using peaceful means

Nelson Mandela: A famous activist from South Africa

Racism: The practice of the belief that one race or group of people is superior to another

Think, Talk and Write

Think About It

Mahatma Gandhi fought for freedom and equality.
What did you like best about Gandhi?
Think about why you liked that best.

Talk About It

Work with a partner who has also read this book.
Make a list of things you would tell him about the time you live in.

Write About It

Gandhi believed in non-violence.
Do you like his idea?
Write a few sentences about your ideas.
Write about other people who used his ideas.

What did you learn from Mahatma Gandhi?

What are the five things that you will change after reading Mahatma Gandhi's story?

A Day With
Martin Luther King, Jr.

Martin Luther King, Jr. was a famous leader and activist.
He fought for the rights of African-American people.
Read on to learn about his life and work.

Martin Luther King, Jr. was born in an **African-American** family in Atlanta, **United States of America** on 15 January, 1929.
He was a famous American leader and activist.

Young Martin Luther King, Jr. liked school.
He was a bright student.
He also loved sports.
Most of all, he enjoyed playing baseball and riding his bicycle.

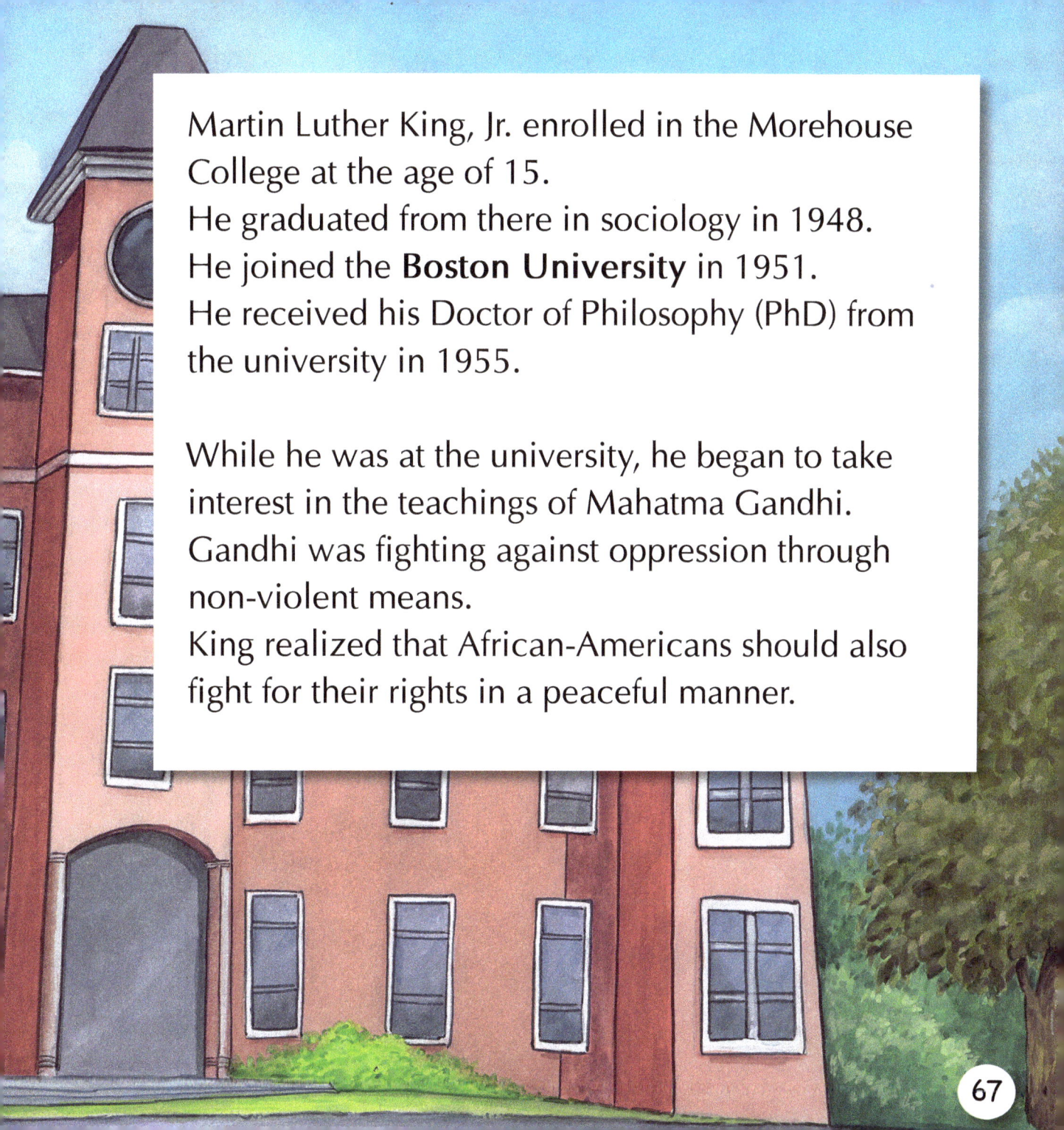

Martin Luther King, Jr. enrolled in the Morehouse College at the age of 15.
He graduated from there in sociology in 1948.
He joined the **Boston University** in 1951.
He received his Doctor of Philosophy (PhD) from the university in 1955.

While he was at the university, he began to take interest in the teachings of Mahatma Gandhi.
Gandhi was fighting against oppression through non-violent means.
King realized that African-Americans should also fight for their rights in a peaceful manner.

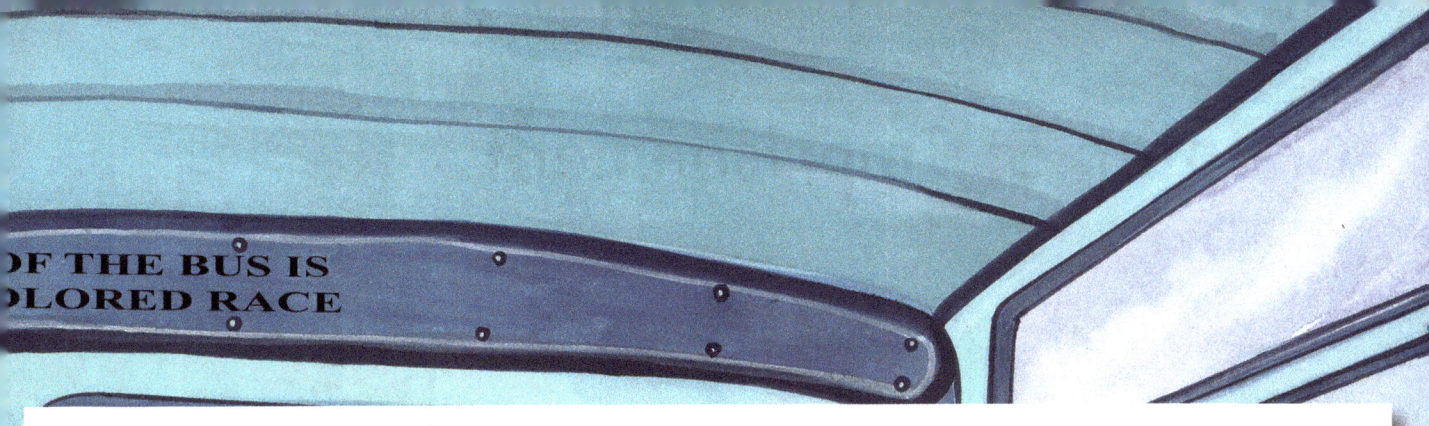

During Martin Luther King, Jr.'s time, African-Americans had few rights. Racism prevailed in America. There was a lot of discrimination. King wanted to fight for African-Americans' rights.

He knew that African-Americans were not allowed to sit with white people in public buses.
African-Americans could sit only at the back seats of buses.
King decided to protest against this **prejudice**.
He called for a boycott of all public buses.
African-Americans refused to travel in public buses.
The boycott lasted for 382 days.

Finally, King got the law changed and African-Americans were allowed to sit along with white people. The boycott was a success.

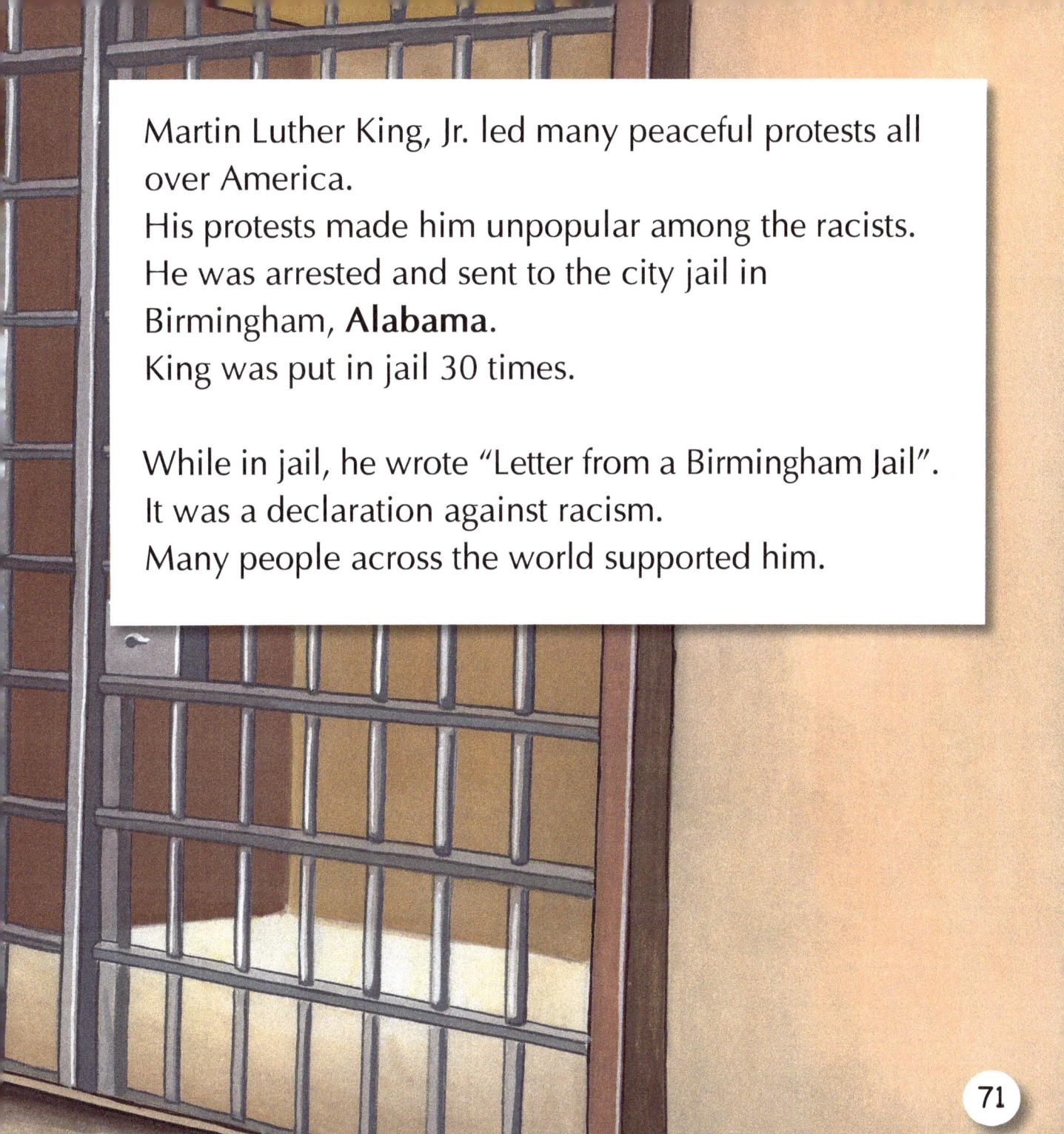

Martin Luther King, Jr. led many peaceful protests all over America.
His protests made him unpopular among the racists.
He was arrested and sent to the city jail in Birmingham, **Alabama**.
King was put in jail 30 times.

While in jail, he wrote "Letter from a Birmingham Jail".
It was a declaration against racism.
Many people across the world supported him.

In 1963, Martin Luther King, Jr. led a protest in **Washington, D.C.**
It was the largest protest in the capital of the United States.
250,000 people took part in it.
Many other leaders also joined him.

King delivered his most famous speech "I have a dream" during the protest.
It is one of the most famous speeches in the world.
He spoke about equality and justice.

Martin Luther King, Jr. won a big prize in 1964.
It was the **Nobel Prize** for Peace.
He won it for his peaceful struggle against racism.

Martin Luther King, Jr. travelled all over the United States.
He gave hundreds of speeches.
People were impressed with his message.
He spoke against hatred and injustice.

King was also an author.
He wrote five books.
His first book was *Stride Toward Freedom: The Montgomery Story*.

Martin Luther King, Jr. was an icon of equality and goodwill. Many schools and streets in the United States are named after him. The third Monday in January each year is celebrated as Martin Luther King, Jr. Day in the United States.

He was assassinated in Memphis, United States on 4 April, 1968.

Timeline

1948
Graduates from
Morehouse College

1929
Born in the
United States

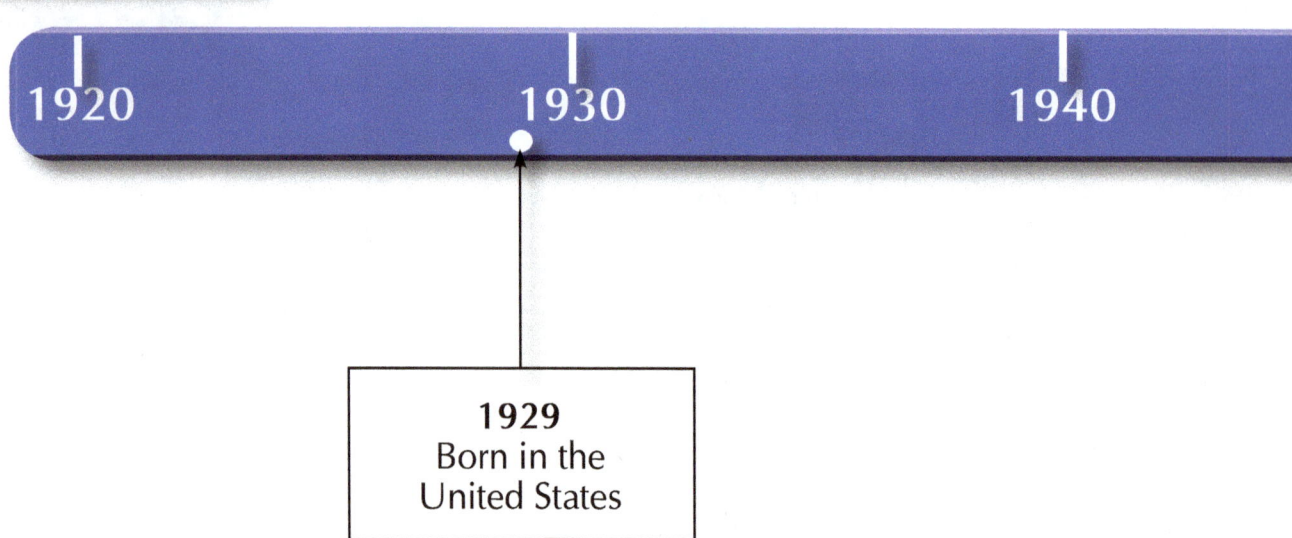

Martin Luther King, Jr.'s Life and Work

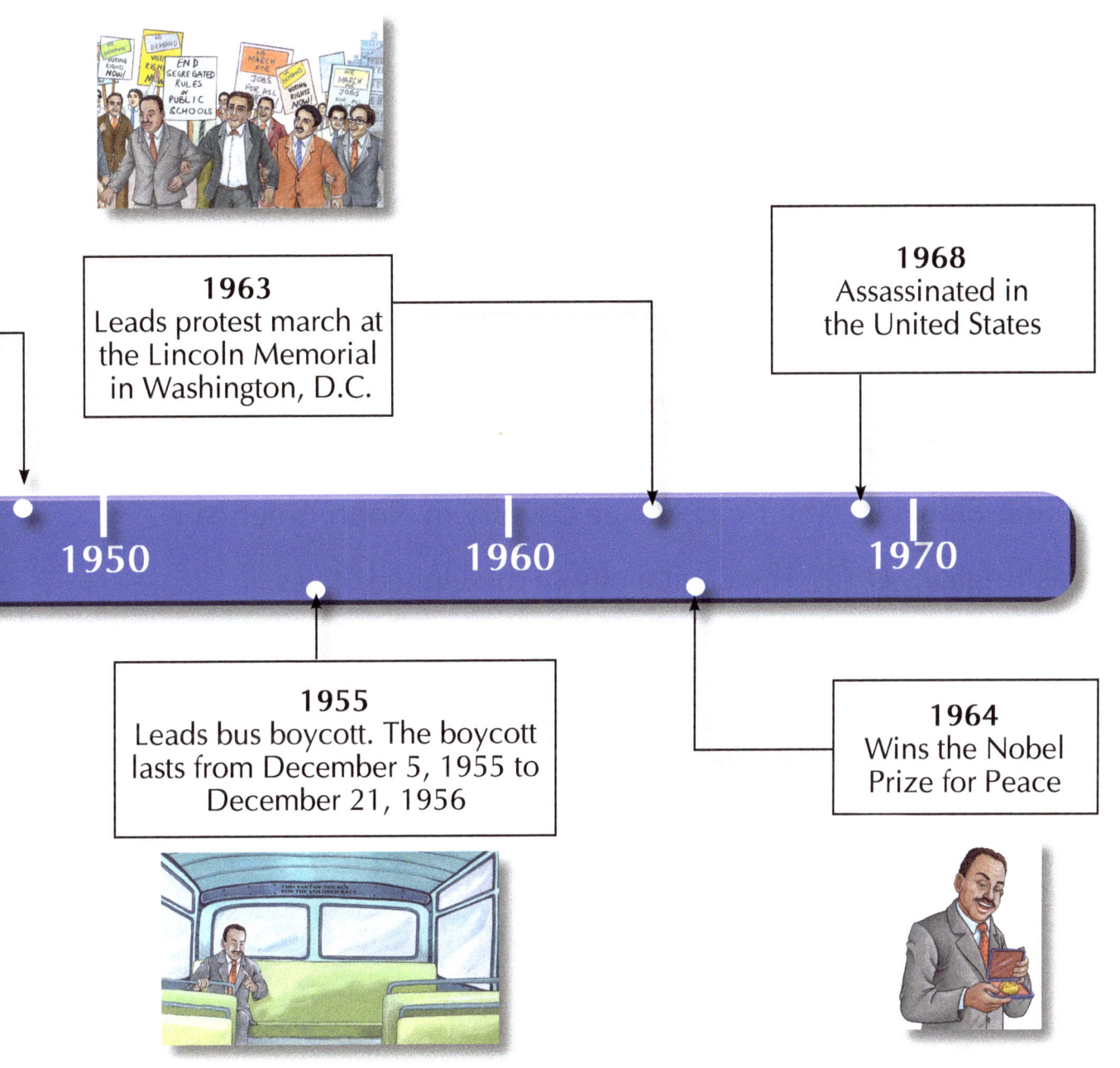

Word Meanings

African-American: An American whose ancestors came from Africa

Alabama: a state in the south-eastern part of the United States

Boston University: A university in Massachusetts

Nobel Prize: A special prize that honours great work

Prejudice: Unreasonable dislike and behaviour towards a particular group of people or things

United States of America: A large country in North America

Washington, D.C.: The capital city of the United States

Think, Talk and Write

Think About It

Martin Luther King, Jr. had a dream.
His dream was that people everywhere would learn to live together without being mean to one another.
What would you do to achieve his dream?
Think about this and explain your answer.

Talk About It

How would you describe Martin Luther King, Jr.?
Tell a friend about him, what he did and how he helped other African-American people.

Write About It

Martin Luther King, Jr. fought for peace and equality.
What would you like to do when you grow up?
Write about what you would like to do and why.

What did you learn from Martin Luther King, Jr.?

What are the five things that you will change after reading Martin Luther King, Jr.'s story?

A Day With

Mother Teresa

Mother Teresa was a famous missionary.
She helped sick and dying people.
Read on to discover about her life and work.

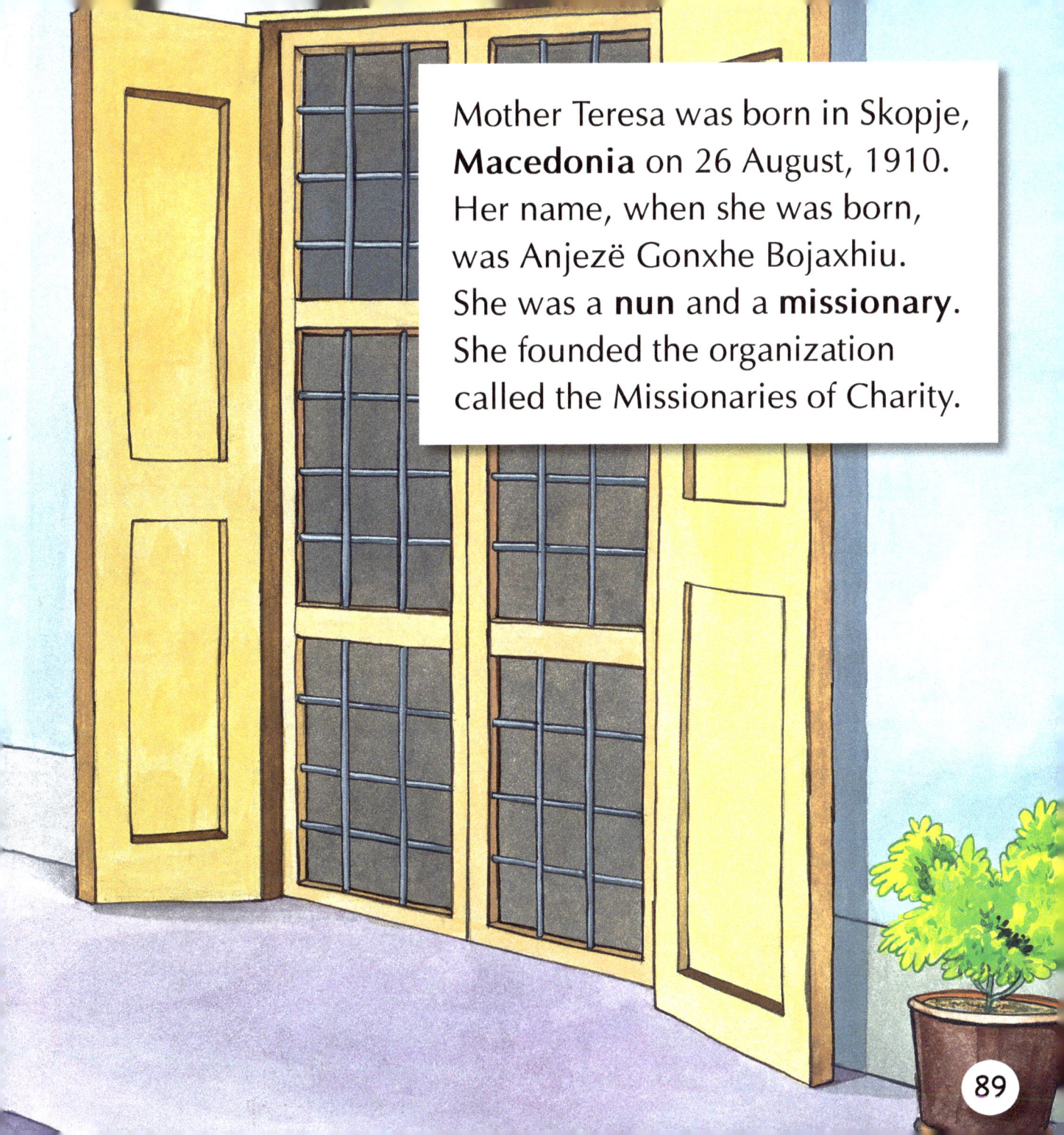

Mother Teresa was born in Skopje, **Macedonia** on 26 August, 1910. Her name, when she was born, was Anjezë Gonxhe Bojaxhiu. She was a **nun** and a **missionary**. She founded the organization called the Missionaries of Charity.

When Mother Teresa was young, she wanted to be a missionary.
So, she joined the Sisters of Loreto.
They are Irish nuns who also worked in India.
She was trained in **Dublin** and sent to India.

Mother Teresa became a teacher in **Calcutta** (now Kolkata). She started teaching at St. Mary's High School. She taught history and geography. Later in 1944, she became the principal of the school.

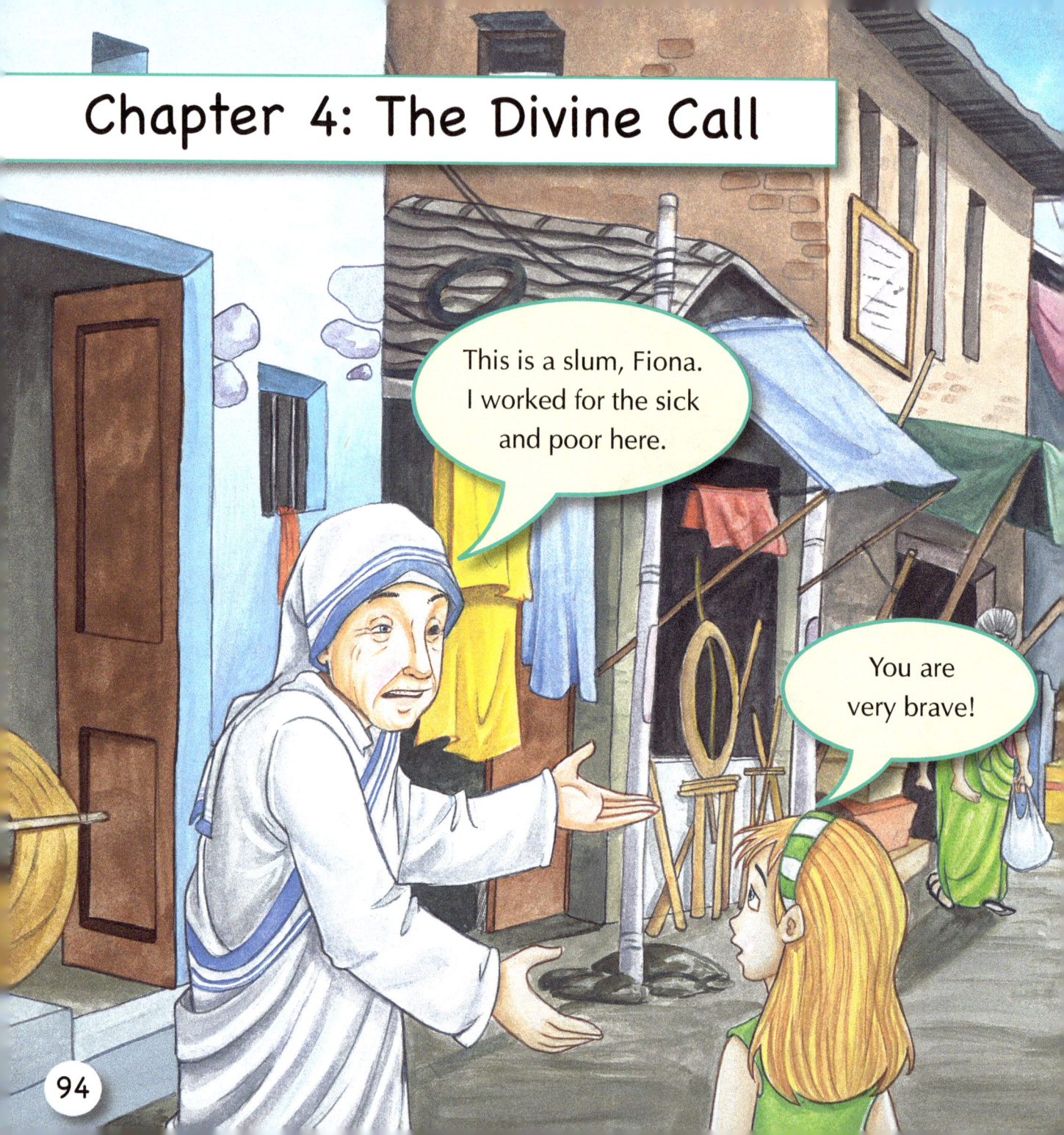

The sick and poor people of Calcutta lived in slums.
Mother Teresa was saddened by the poverty she saw in the slums.
In 1946, she fell ill. She was sent to the hills to recover from her illness.
On the journey, she felt a **divine** call from within herself.
It asked her to care for the sick and poor.
In 1948, she left St. Mary's High School.
She began to work among the sick and poor in the slums of Calcutta to help them get better.

Mother Teresa learned basic medicine.
She nursed sick and dying people.
She also taught poor children.

In 1949, her former students joined her.
They rented a room to care for sick, old and dying people.
The next year, she named this group the 'Missionaries of Charity'.

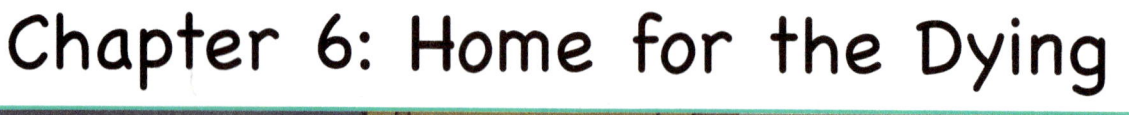

In 1952, Mother Teresa opened a home for the dying in a temple in Calcutta.
Later, it was renamed 'Nirmal Hriday'—Home of the Pure Heart.
She brought sick and dying people to her home.
She gave them medicine. She took care of them.
She prayed for them.

Mother Teresa wanted to help more people.
She went to **Africa** to feed the hungry.
She also went to many other places to help the needy.
She set up 450 help centres around the world.

Mother Teresa won a big prize in 1979.
It was the **Nobel Prize** for Peace.
She won it for working for sick and poor people.

Mother Teresa was full of kindness and love. She was a messenger of peace.

Mother Teresa died in Kolkata, India on 5 September, 1997.

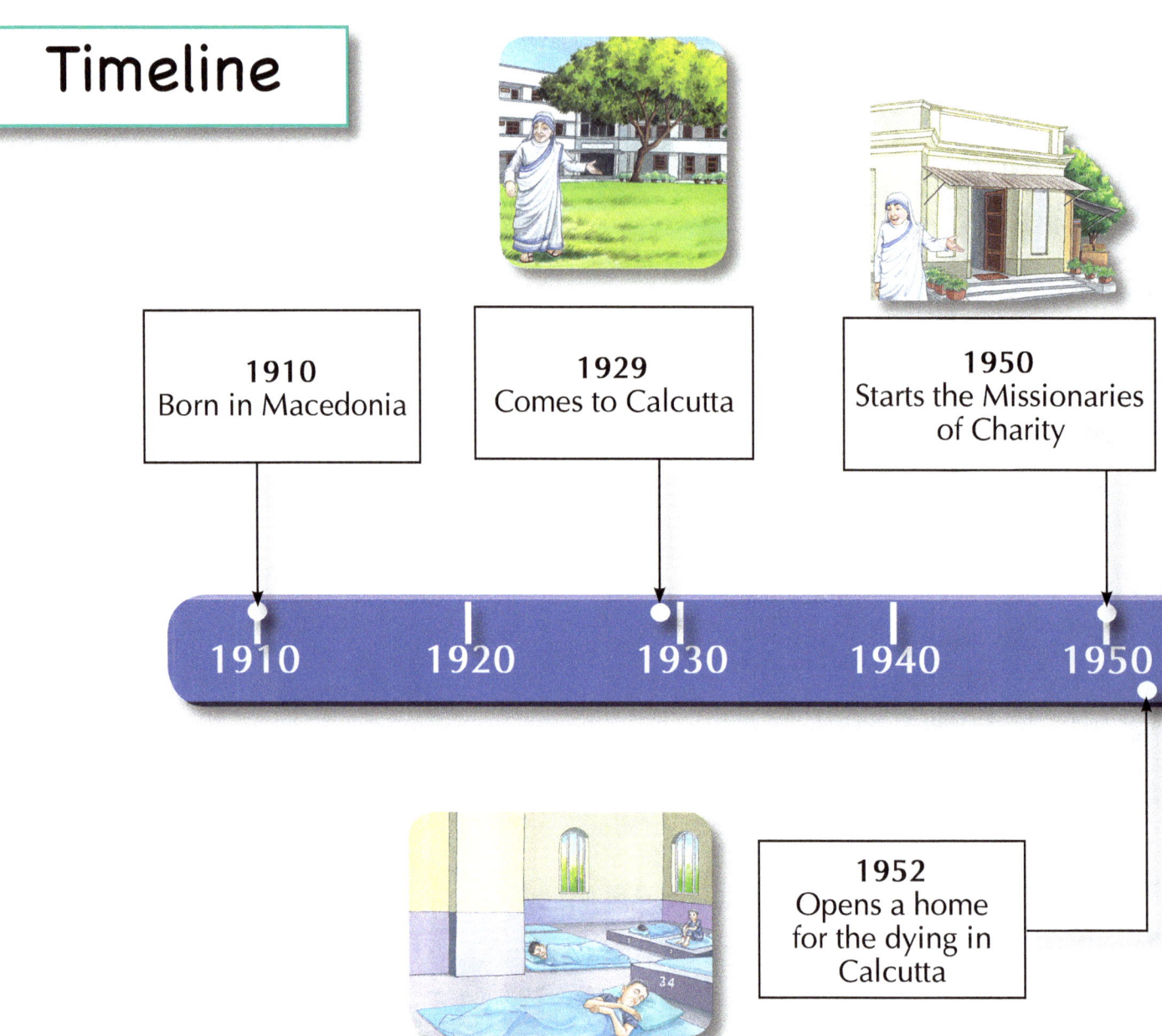

Timeline

Mother Teresa's Life and Work

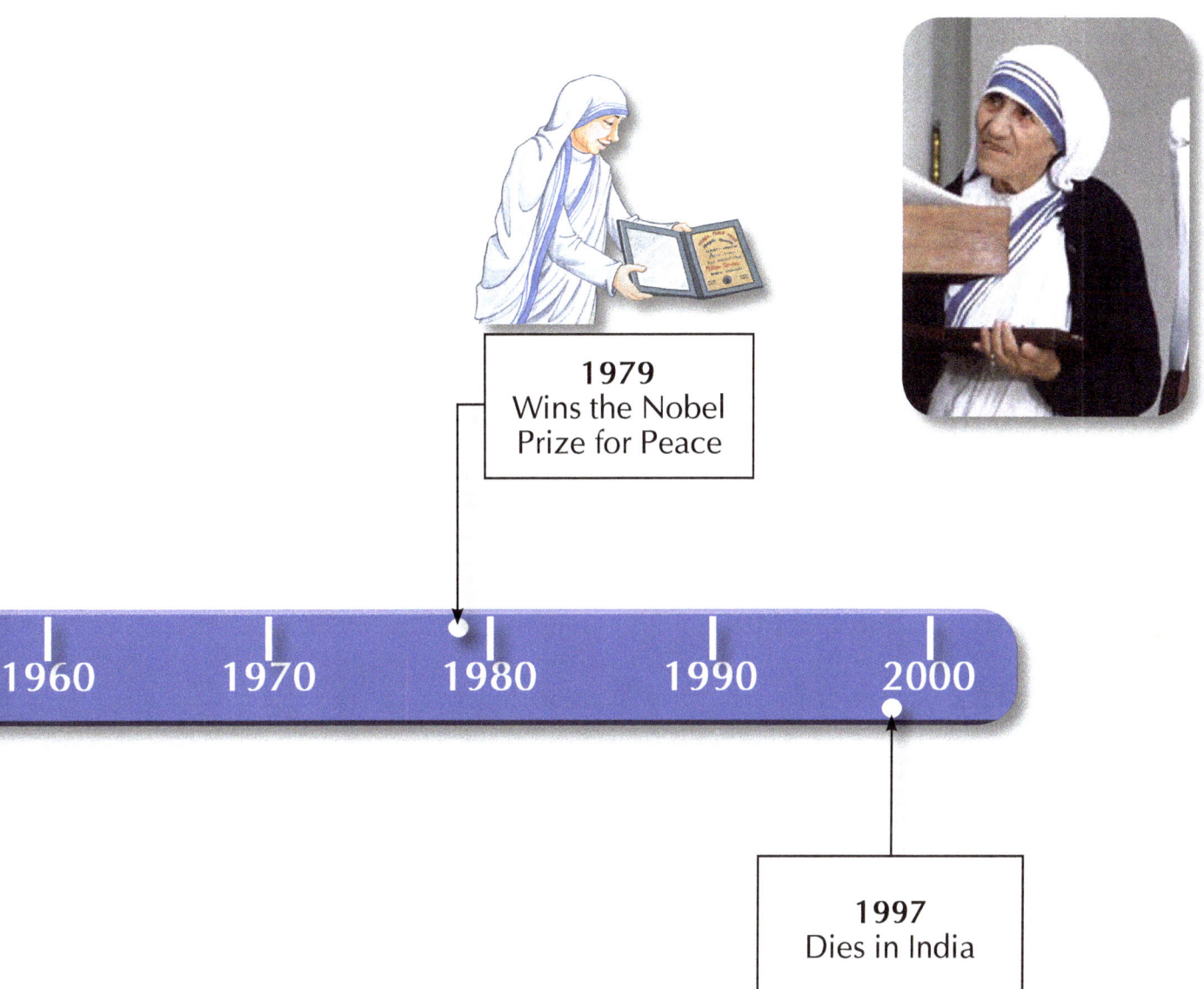

1979
Wins the Nobel Prize for Peace

1997
Dies in India

Word Meanings

Africa: The second largest continent to the south of the Mediterranean Sea, to the east of the Atlantic Ocean and to the west of the Indian Ocean

Calcutta: A city in Eastern India. Calcutta is now known as Kolkata

Divine: Relating to or proceeding directly from God or a god

Dublin: A city in Ireland. Dublin is the capital of Ireland

Macedonia: A country in Southeastern Europe, north of Greece

Missionary: A person who chooses to serve people of other cultures, usually in a foreign country

Nobel Prize: A special prize that honours great work.

Nun: A religious woman who has taken special vows and usually lives in convents

Think, Talk and Write

Think about It

How did Mother Teresa become a missionary?
Think of a list of things that she did as a missionary.

Talk about It

What interests you most about Mother Teresa? Tell family or friends about her.
Explain to them what interests you most about Mother Teresa. Talk about other things you learned about her.

Write about It

Mother Teresa wanted to be a missionary.
What would you like to be?
Write a few sentences about what you would like to be when you grow up and why.

What did you learn from Mother Teresa?

What are the five things that you will change after reading Mother Teresa's story?

Work Space

www.ingramcontent.com/pod-product-compliance
Lightning Source LLC
Chambersburg PA
CBHW062132160426
43191CB00013B/2278